Back C

Kathleen Mcphilemy

Littoral Press

First published 2022 by
Littoral Press, 15 Harwood Place,
Lavenham, Sudbury, Suffolk CO10 9SG

ISBN 978-1-912412-41-9

British Library Cataloguing-in-Publication Data:
A catalogue record of this book is available from
The British Library

Printed and bound in Great Britain by
4Edge Ltd. Hockley, Essex
www.4edge.co.uk

Also by Kathleen Mcphilemy:

The Lion in the Forest (Katabasis, 2004)

A Tented Peace (Katabasis, 1995)

A Witness to Magic (Hearing Eye, 1990)

Kathleen McPhilemy was born in Belfast where she grew up. She has lived in London, Edinburgh and Oxford, where she taught in Further Education until her retirement.

Acknowledgements:

Some of these poems have previously appeared in *Acumen, Agenda, Dreamcatcher, The Cannon's Mouth, The High Window, Honest Ulsterman, Ink, Sweat and Tears, London Grip, The SHop, Sofia.*

'Blue Girl' was published in the anthology, *Hands and Wings,* (White Rat Press, 2015)

'Cassandra' appeared in the anthology, *Rebel Talk* (Oxford Extinction Rebellion, 2021)

Contents

I

II

IV

V

I

Bonamargy Friary

How long does it take till history settles
like old tombstones in a grey landscape?
forgotten place of lost golfballs
and tall nettles, sanitised now
with mown pathways, a heritage site
twirly lettering.

MacDonnells and McQuillans
raged over these fields
battles betrayals treachery anguish
but dissolution was late here
Franciscan friars provided shelter
for recusants and Scottish Catholics.

Place of war, place of worship
did it die slowly or in a night of fire?
In my mind, I see the last friar
a grey man on the Grey Man's path
precipitous descent of basalt cliffs
to the lesser terror of the roiling sea.

Back Country

On these half-known roads
between the city and the sea
grey condenses on the grass
colours fade from the fields
trees transform to shadowy signallers.

In farms and cottages
at the ends of rough lanes
lights wink on
in the imaginable comfort
of other houses, other lives.

What is not imagined
is the later darkness
cars without plates or lights
sweep into a farmyard
hard men step out.

What is not imagined
are the few words spoken
what they take with them
what they leave behind
under the tarpaulin.

Home

'Not from round here, are you?'
'I was born here,' you say.
They look at you, disbelievingly:
'You've been gone too long
you've travelled too far
your accent is wrong
you were never from here,'
they think, but don't say.

Pub on the junction
between city and coast
never stopped there
people and music
nowhere to park
bad people drink there
bad things are planned
go in and they watch you
from the door to the bar.

They know who you are
(even if you don't)
driving past
from safe spot to safe spot
never from here
wherever you are.

Medbh McGuckian's Cottage

It was your garden after all
the rainy days we walked there
poked round the outside
could never see in

hortus conclusus
you walled up with words
impenetrable and never
the place where those messages

were sent and received
not as purported
but you kept the sea
as your open frontier

listened to its stories
and the rabble of stones.

Truth and Reconciliation

Two old men
mobiles on loud speaker
shouting down the line
their same old stories

come to me afterwards
their raucous whispers
curdle and burn
in the porch of my ear

otherwise you
in your poison garden
your array of amphorae
sealed and painted

bright abstractions of ancient tales
occlude the festering histories inside.

Sicilia

Sausages

Colin Glen pork sausages from Ireland

All changed now
I couldn't find my way
what with the peace walls
and street names in Irish

mostly it's the lettering
words are the same
where I thought I knew
turned inside out

Colin Hill Colin Glen
truckloads of squealers
the hills hold their secrets
so does the abattoir

hard to see what's going on
further up or down the road.

No Surrender

All the queen's seahorses won't take it from me:
sand and the sunset path on the water,
dunes I have trodden, yellow archangel,
oystercatcher margin where I placed my ante,
closer than that gave all to the tide.

All of it named in a half-hidden language,
fragments of fragments, forgotten stories,
medleys of memories: salt sea coal
caves and tunnels and rusting jetties
sliding sideways under seagulls into the sea.

Once there was a railway and habited nuns,
forbidden flirtation on the links, on the rocks
there were bathing boxes, boys in togs
poised for the camera, face carved in stone
under an impossible inaccessible brow.

However far inland she chooses to bury me
I will always be there: rain on her windows,
squawk of the gulls, spume from the waves,
light that winks and blinks from the island,
rattle of pebbles on the shore below.

Rip tides

Deirdre McShane: drowned on Ballycastle Beach, 9th December, 2019.

I could be standing barefoot
at the mouth of the Margy
toes curled into
the cold wet sand
where the river meets
the churn of the waves
and children play
in the swirling shallows

suddenly snatched
by the conflict of waters
they're rolled and tumbled
until passers-by
wade through the foam
the spume and the froth
grab them and drag them
back to the shore

and I could have been there
when the helicopter landed
above on the links
on the seventh fairway;
I could have watched
paramedics lumber
to wrap the children
in warm red blankets
or the foil they use
for hypothermia.

So many years earlier
the boys on the pier
sunlight glinting
on their smooth bare chests
on the chains of their crucifixes
on their dripping hair
dived and surfaced
supple as mackerel
that swam beneath them
nosing limpets and weed;

I could have been told
how a great wave came
over the seawall, swept
off a fisherman, how a boy
leapt in, pulled him to safety
went home for his tea
late, was told off
but never said anything
so long ago
it's not even on Google.

I could have been there
with those morning swimmers
I could have been passing
walking my dog
(I don't have a dog)
I could have been there
near the mouth of the Margy
at the candlelit vigil
but I wasn't and it isn't
my place to grieve.

II

Behind the Wall

Over and over, the backdrop of flowers
gives way to darkness. Behind the wall
red brick, green ivy, darkness is waiting
for appearance to fail and to fall.

Over and over, a voice with a gun
comes into the house, the walls fall away
then there is only the whispering darkness
hot breath, and bodies you didn't see.

Over and over, death in the darkness
whispered by voices you must believe
you cannot trust, over and over
flowers deceive, walls fall away.

Another, someone, you

shadow faces rising from the pavements
everywhere are my fear
whisper of other languages
in doorways, in buildings I don't belong in
the new is what I'm afraid of
in bedrooms I shouldn't be in
children of the new age
the news is what I'm afraid of
all God's children except
I no longer believe in God and
the boundaries of human are blurring
are they brothers or sisters
if they want to kill
not me personally
they don't even see me

as it always was, political
I might deny my own but another's
is disrespectful
another, someone, you
if you come at me with a sword
and the blinding sun behind you
all you will see are my clothes
all I will see is your sword

but I can't put God in the dustbin
god(s) we have made that have shaped us
gods they have made for survival
in the heat and sand of the desert
so cruel in the name of mercy
where is the god of rain
there is a god who is always weeping

so many wrong decisions
in the muddy ditches of sorrow
no climbing out into sunlight
no surge into life with the spring
though grass is no longer a symbol
of more than matter and death

belief entwined inside
like a spinal cord articulates
all that you do and say
how should I disconnect you
how would I have the right
what have I got to offer
uncertainty, unbelief
I am slow-footed to follow
the dizzying whirl of change

what does a chimpanzee think
when does a foetus feel pain
how different are sex and gender
whose hand is holding the knife
the syringe, the packets of pills
are you a boy or a girl
do you have a father and mother
or either or other or both
do the questions even make sense
do I have the right to ask
another or someone or you
no longer out there somewhere else
but here implicit inside me
folded into my veins and my blood.

Coming or going

Three covered shapes on the hill or horizon
against a backdrop of black or orangey-red
one standing, one stooping, one on her knees;
-they seem to be women by the figures they cut
from the fabric of dawn or sunset or war.

It's hard to tell if they're coming or going
or static forever on that liminal line;
teenagers seeking hope in the desert
or refugees stumbling away from the fire:
whoever they are, they are not like us.

Girls together plotting in the playground
late at night in the light of their screens
caught on camera hauling their trolley bags
from airport to airport - why not heroic?-
helping each other from buses and trains.

Or widows, old women, exhausted mothers
stopping perhaps on their way towards us
to rest, to pray, to bury a child;
if they make it here over sand and sea
how can we think we will understand them?

Privilege

Wooden doors centuries thick
knuckle-duster studded

beyond them are stairways
beyond them are gardens

wonderful rooms of gold and marble
damask and crystal

the keys are weighty
thick as your arm

they are only used
from the inside.

Pietà

She holds his body in her arms,
the body she holds is a man's body
beard still growing, skin leathered
toenails strong but chipped from walking
muscles and sinews even now defined
beautiful, rigid, withdrawing into marble.

There were harsh words between them
he grew up and away from her
intolerant of her not understanding;
she turned also, hid her hurt
stored it along with the joyful memories,
the innocence, all her service.

She can remember his boy's body
the child's face, clear, unblemished,
his smooth brown skin sparkling with water drops,
how she held him and dried him,
how he relaxed against her
when he was still hers.

Orestes

Everyone who has been in a war
even a small war, even at second hand,
knows it has changed their life.

Everyone who has been in a war
knows how doors close,
how borders are created and close,
how the phone goes
too late at night.

Everyone who has been in a war
knows who they know they don't know
learns to keep silent
learns to distrust the daylight
learns the language of darkness
becomes a creature of darkness.

Everyone who has been in a war
believes there was another life
the life they should have had
a life of daylight and trust and long heart-to-hearts
with friends, without borders;
but everyone who has been in a war
knows that is just sentimental.

Everyone who has been in a war
struggles with now and the future
can't relinquish the selves
that were lost when lives were lost
that died when trust was murdered
that were betrayed by the failure of justice.

The past is the land of the dead
of vengeful and poisonous shadows
of furies posing as friends;
Everyone who has been in a war
has to deal with survival.

Don't want to know

Behind that man always another
dark shadow against a yellow wall
his left hand holding high
a hammer
a sword
a gun
a book

the other hand
beckons us forward
is it me
is it you
is it us
is it all of us

a cavern a tunnel gapes open behind him
Here is the truth he whispers
in his telephone voice
here is the truth. Sh, sh
shadows and darkness.

Half way

Perhaps we are half way
at least we are away
after paying the smugglers
we are left with nothing
they say we are in Europe
but we are still a long way
from anywhere we want to be.

You are halfway to summer
nearly all the way to spring
where you live the climate
always reassures you
the wheel of the seasons
always comes round.

For you today
the sun was warm
where we used to live
it was always hot;
here it is raining
and there's a forecast of rain
for a monthful of days.

When it began our children weren't born
now parents, uncles, sisters have died.
Those who have stayed ask
"When will it be over?"
Those who have left:
'When will we get there?'
What kind of an answer is
'Half way'?

Vowel Sounds

I have not lost my language
nor travelled to a far city
to live among strangers;

I have not been reduced
to the status of a slow-witted child
because I cannot shop or tell the time.

I have lost my accent
or at least the innocence
of thinking that all the world
shared my vowel sounds.

So I know a little how it feels
in a street, or a bus or waiting room
when the ear vibrates to a certain way of speaking
that must be someone from home.

Losing Children
(Annotations on Blake's *Songs of Innocence)*

Border

Razor wire green grass

                     children at play

having a kickabout

                 laughter daylight

and the guards are smiling:

                         it's the double perspective:

for shepherd as for sheep

                     the lorries are waiting

he keeps them safe

             till the end of summer

then counts them up the ramp

                   and slams the tailgate

he signals to the driver

             "That's the way it is".

Lost daughter

She checks her phone again -
how can she sleep
when the concave space
she keeps beside her heart
is empty?
She checks her phone again –
she has no faith
she fears the desert
the lion's claws are bloody.
She checks her phone again –
how could she trust her child
to smooth-tongued men
the lascivious smiles of strangers?
She checks her phone again.

Travelworn

Benighted on this border
                  beneath flimsy canvas
coloured tents compete
                  with liveried trains
that will not stop for you
                  but nudge ungently.

These tracks, trains, guards
                  home no longer is
my little worn-out shoe
                  dream the stories
your mother used to tell
                  of loving fathers;
sleep dream
                  if you're not too cold and hungry.

Sweepers

London sparrows are cheeky in the ivy;
all little boys are different.
This one,
          with his straight dark hair
his olive stone eyes
                    his voice like the solo line
in a clarinet concerto
                    is chimney fodder

so many spilt children
                    miscarried babies:
silent mothers
                    absent fathers
robin redbreasts
                    are sobbing in the ivy.

48 hours

Unborn
uncut
no page opened
possibilities
permutations
only guessed at
two days and not even
safely berthed

Uncut
I happy am
my inmost tender
secret self
keep from the knife
its sharp distinction

Othering

He doesn't exist
that darker brother;
even Blake got it wrong
when he looked in the mirror
and saw himself
his own good nature.

As for that other
we don't have a name for
he'll not incline
to shade and protect us
from the fierce and shrivelling
force we created
when we carried away
so much that he had.

Stateless

The brown-faced boy in the garden
is shooting down cherry-blossoms;
like tiny perfections of marble
they fall to the ground and shatter.

The bare-foot boy in the garden
has walked here on a path of splinters,
the bones and the homes of his parents;
a splinter has lodged in his heart.

The bare-faced boy in the garden
is too young to remember before
when olive and almond trees
flowered and then bore fruit.

Back then

Names, borders, the lie of the land,
there was knowing and not knowing
villages flattened to make a garden
drowned houses, pleasure lakes.

There was knowing and not knowing
who trimmed the hedges, dug the gardens,
why there were places you couldn't go
children you didn't play with.

Ravaged by knowledge, that old landscape,
where the scent of the neighbour's jasmine
drifted to your window, will never recover
or smell simply of jasmine again.

Existential Dread

What are they all so scared of?
Bugs from the east nuclear war games
melting ice floes rising waters
desertification disappearance of species

I stay calm
my house is on the high ground
my family is well
and I shut out the news

but I hug to myself
my dark red comforter
the nameless terror
that keeps me awake

alert and uncomfortably
perched on the moment.

Catching our Breath *(Spring, 2020)*

Easter Sunday and predictably
Jesus has risen; predictably
the gardens are full of blossom
and on the path by the park
catkins are greeny and silver;
less predictably, the skies
are clean and clear and empty
the playground is locked and empty;
the weekend has been breathtakingly lovely
for those with breath for the taking.

Utterly strange and changed:
do we miss the engine of capitalism
now that it has stuttered and stopped?
We look towards summer and autumn
for normal to come back but normal
may be a normal utterly changed:
we have seen the goodness of people
and we have seen the lies of a government
that disregarded its scientists
and was happy for the weakest to die.

Under the sun an enormous quietness;
out of the sun, predictably
an increase in hatred and violence
enclosed in narrowing walls;
less predictably, acts of kindness
everywhere from ordinary people;
and behind those doors that are closed
out of sight of the healthy
shut away from the sun
extraordinary acts of courage.

Drifting in this strange narcosis
don't we know who is dying? -
the expendable old, replaceable carers
the pickers, the packers, the drivers
the cleaners, the orderlies, the porters
underpaid and underprotected
while the privileged work from home;
don't we know this was predicted
and ignored to get Brexit done?

Unpredictable when and how we will rise
unpredictable if and how we will change:
will we learn to reward the ordinary
to build homes for ordinary heroes
make space for all to breathe?
Probably not; much more likely
patched up with some bodged repairs
the machine will lurch into action
backwards to the City of Destruction
backwards with all flags waving.

Inside Out

When the broad beans failed to germinate
I poked my finger into the compost;
down there, something was happening
but later a kiss of mildew
appeared like guilt on the surface.
Insides should never be seen:
the finger, the forensic knife
is always a violation.

So when the wrecker's ball lays open
the upper storeys of buildings
right at the heart of the city
and all who pass can stare
at the intimacy of abandoned wallpaper
at the doorframe wrenched awry
our innards shiver and cringe
at such casual berserker violence.

III

One for sorrow

St Valentine's Day and now
it is we who are falling
one by one all around
in spring sunshine is the glitter
of a magpie's eye
he fixes me
from his perch on the half-wrecked shed
auguring this week's sorrow

fresh in black and white finery
he lifts over the raised beds
flirts and jinks
over the late-standing leeks
and shoots of garlic poking through
the dark turned over earth.

What Makes Cherry Blossom Pink?

Someone I imagine is staring out
across the grey lines of undulating tiles
on low-rise rooftops. Saved daylight
and for the first time the tree reveals
itself and she believes in spring again;
its trunk is branchless till it crests the buildings
in horizontal swathes of cherry blossom
she knows is pink, even in the gloaming.

Flavanoids are a class of plant and fungus
secondary metabolites, colouring petals
attract pollinators in trees and flowers
red/blue pigmentation, pinks and purples;

or rods and cones in the eye of the beholder
who needs the tree and everything it stands for.

Archaeopteryx

Diving into layers of old gold,
muzzle and forepaws, dog digs deeper
where autumn drifts against tree roots,
disturbs the fragile bone cages,
skeletal remnants of dead things -
rat, squirrel or a fallen bird;

leaves decay like a child's painting,
all those colours to dirty brown
meld with the flesh of small cadavers
rotting down to a forest mulch.

Was it like this or was it more conscient digging
uncovered the exquisitely etched feather
or the old wing of the Ur Vogel,
encrypted data of time before time
when tiny dinosaurs flapped their overcoats
took to the air in powered flight?

Wintry clouds lour on the treeline,
darkness draws down on these late days.
Can we imagine ourselves as fossils,
incised in rocks still unformed,
excavated by chance or purposeful quest?
Can we imagine the light in their eyes
as they gaze at our relics freighted with meaning?

Noisy Squawkers

I saw the parakeets yesterday
where I knew they would be
in the park near the riverbank
flashing from tree to tree.

How out of place they are
with their bright green feathers
their long foreign tails
and their raucous blether.

I have searched all spring
for the blue of the kingfisher
and I yearn for the ratcheting
cry of the corncrake

I heard as a child
lying on top of the single haystack
in the scrubby field
behind our house.

But now it's parakeets
confronting with valour
and noisy cheerfulness
the cold wet of our winters.

Let them stay
like the rabbit and grey squirrel
configure our landscape
become unremarkable.

Context

This budgie on the allotment
doesn't belong
the dejection of his shoulders
drooping wings
show that he knows
he's the wrong colour
his beak is the wrong shape
he is altogether out of place.

If only
someone would come with a cage
put it beside him
on the ground
with a bell and a mirror and a millet spray
he would hop in
everyone would relax and
he would be ok.

The Gentle Bush*

There you are: lurking in plain sight
not even at the bottom of my garden;
the birds and squirrels know you and at night
the fox will seek your shelter, dodge the moon.
Shaggy, disregarded, a briar rose
climbs through you and little cabbage whites,
my brother once called fairies, flutter at your base;
beneath our walls the tangle of your roots
snakes and coils so slowly a century might pass.
Centuries have passed since this was last a field
where dancers circled, shadows in the grass,
whom only poachers saw and all that told
that they had been, their only residue
those darker rings under the morning dew.

The hawthorn

Red Kite

The kite is a civilised bird,
it has followed us up the M40;
feasting on bins and roadkill
it has thrived and multiplied.

One circles above the tall trees
at the far end of the allotments;
as sunlight catches its underwing
there is a flashing awareness of red;

sometimes it perches on a high branch,
resting or waiting and watching
the bustling rabbit metropolis
in the adjoining nature reserve

reclaimed from a city landfill,
raised above the river by rubbish.
The saplings have grown into trees,
there are owls and snipe and cuckoos

and above them again, the kite
climbs and wheels and drifts
in a casual mastery of air
that is something quite different from freedom.

Moorhen

Not so much hen
more shaped like a pullet
not so much moor
more of a rivulet

that's where I see you
red beak, white tail feathers
between allotment hedge
and bridge over the railway

the trains are your weather
natural, quotidian
as sunshine and rainstorm

swimming upstream and downstream
you are mostly solitary
in your private wilderness.

5th March, 2018

Hanging out the laundry for the first time
I spotted a robin under the gooseberry bush
perky, prompt as a court jester
alert for cues.

The last heaps of snow lay on the verges
on the way to the garage
like children in body bags
but daffodils and crocuses have made it through
they always do.

Coming back from the vet, I felt the cat
shift in the carrier, his last spring.
Just one of my trays of early cabbages
has sprouted. I peeked in
when I brought back the laundry out of the rain.

Cassandra

The woman is slim, young, soldier straight;
she strains her shoulders backwards
against the straps of the baby sling
though the baby is still so new
its arms and legs barely protrude;
the man's spine curves the other way
his burden the rucksack of baby necessities
nappies, wipes, a bottle, the just-in-case
full set of clothes; their companion
another woman carries nothing and her long
curly hair lifts behind her.

Such a beautiful day they have come to the rec
the playground they are still not quite entitled to;
they sit on a bench to feel sunlight on skin
escape from claustrophobic hours in the dark
sleeplessness, the insatiable recurrences
their child has introduced them to;
relaxed, reassured they can taunt their friend
with the tiny perfections of fingers and toes
the yearning tenderness evoked by any small mammal
challenge her choice, her earth-saving earnestness
decision not to have children.

Such a beautiful spring they hardly notice
cuckoos are absent, bats do not fly
swifts arc and wheel in reducing numbers.
She sits beside them, marking all this
files it along with other horrors
she knows they'd rather she didn't talk about;
she lets her hair droop round her face
like tattered curtains to the world's future

while across the park busy house martins
come and go from the eaves of the newbuilds
behind the wall, beside the lane to the meadow.

Caroline's Tree

Those nights, the gracious acacia
would draw itself on the window
and, although the wind could be heard,
the wind didn't stir its branches;
Then, I would swing from my bedroom
on green, imagined lianas
to a distant and vertical city,
a shifting and different polity
of woodpeckers, finches and pigeons,
squirrels, blackbirds and starlings.

When I looked at Caroline's tree
in all its many phases
and different stages of light
I wished I had been an artist,
to pick out the gold and the black
as the sun revolved through its branches
to record the black and white and red
of the woodpecker nipping up insects
grey and white curves of the pigeons
voluptuous on higher branches
the different grey of squirrels
daring on their high trapeze
goldfinches hidden in green
till they dared to come to the feeder
red and black and yellow.

Its leaves did not come early:
when other trees had stickily
broken out leaves and blossom
it stood austere and skeletal;
but through the summer and autumn

when all the rest had turned dry
carpeting the lawn in yellow
it stayed green and flourishing.

I looked to the gracious acacia
as an emblem of consolation
for the days of rawness and bruising;
but today it holds out wordless
the still bright scars of the chainsaw;
maimed and mutilated arms
where twigs and leaves should ramify.
Cutting it down to the size
of our walls and houses and gardens
they have laid waste the visionary city;
what remains is ordinary daylight.

Bats

The last one I ever saw
was so small, light like a leaf
dried up, its limbs and wings
the design of itself.

Five summers now without them
the sky empty at dusk
and the swifts that darted and circled
in the higher air, also fewer.

But it's the bats I miss most
their different, shadowy lives
dwelling among us quietly
harming no-one.

Willow Boughs at Kelmscott

In the cool of the evening
Mr Morris walks in his garden
Mr Morris of Morris and Co
walks past the medlars and quinces
down to a bend in the river
where he picks up a spray from the willow
the winds tore down in the storm.

Through the symmetries of the vegetable beds
and the less symmetrical orchard
he goes in through the kitchen door
where he gives the willow to May
or Jenny or perhaps it is Jane
to put in a vase or a jar
"Make what you can of that."

May looks out of her attic window
to honour the flowering plums
the white and abundant branches
the surging curve of the blossom
from which line and form are abstract
the ground and source of her art
they are like nothing except themselves.

She will go downstairs in the morning
she will study the spray of willow
the intertwining of twigs and leaves
symmetrical and less symmetrical
she will create a repeating pattern
every 52 centimetres
for wallpaper, curtains and tiles.

Exit West

(after Mohsin Hamid)

Secret roads, tunnels for toads,
drainpipe escapes for otters and others,
over the highway transcendent skyway,
 a dormouse bridge like swaying gossamer;

all across the landscape, slithering and sliding
scurrying of paws, clicking of claws –
all across the landscape, barriers and borders,
metal, concrete, deserts of blacktop.

They came with their ordnance, their mattocks, their axes
everyday sounds were crushed by explosions
blasting the hills, flattening shelters
the rumble of tracks overwhelming birdsong.

Shivering, defenceless, erinacea europea
scuttled and stuttered with her offspring around her
dazed in the ruins of all she had known
starved in a waste of rubble and asphalt.

Then someone had a bright idea:
corridors of safety for these blameless collaterals.
Hedgehogs survive in decreasing numbers
building new lives in alien lands.

IV

Hand in hand
(for KFG)

Whisper of ash, finger of bone
hand that once I held in my own

sound of the sea sound of the wind
dune grass whip   damp sand

I've been here before let me come back
your ring on my finger your veins in my hand
your face in my mirror let me go back

escarpment, island, lights in the bay
shadow of Scotland furthest away

elegant swimmer you have swum from the shore
threading the breakers till I see you no more.

Disoriented

I had been dreaming, now that I'd graduated,
I'd rent a flat somewhere in the city
and live a life of full artistic freedom,

when I remembered the body in the bed
breathing beside me and our several children;

then dozed again, then woke again more fully
to know they all were gone and when I turned
the left side of the bed was silent, empty;
I heard a bumbling in another room
and guessed he'd got up, gone to the toilet.

I forced myself awake, afraid to sleep then wake
to find the bed had narrowed, sheets were chill,
and downstairs noise, the thumps and bumps and crashes
came from carers, plating up the breakfasts,
hoovering the lounge, lining up the chairs
for endless hours of daytime television.

Butterfly

Like a brooch or a bloodstain suddenly there
fluttering on a towel pegged out on the line;
I rushed inside for my naturalist app.
When I got back it was gone so I picked some figs
ripe and yielding. I thought about guilt
and hidden redness and wasps in the garden.

A Red Admiral or Painted Lady?
somehow it seemed redder than those;
think the difference between scarlet and crimson
distinction of venous from arterial blood;
baleful and blameful, token of shame
how shocking the splotch of red is on white!

But red in the end is swallowed by black
surrender to dark that turns the sun
into the Sunday of church interiors
into the guilt of stained glass windows
a furtive uncomfortable leaking of innocence -
unreachable light on untouchable waves.

Blue Girl

(for Rebecca and her parents)

Blue girl
dancing on the rim of darkness,
your spangled blue dress
the empty promise of stars.

Your eye-shadow forecast your weather:
purple was challenging, stormy;
green was sullen, morose
while blue was hyper and happy
skittering across the campus
and the glitter as always was change.

The wood was polished and golden,
light streamed in from the window,
and your coffin also was light,
bright, covered with flowers.

Here is the trick of appearance,
darkness is locked inside;
eyes just closed for a moment,
and you sank through the well-oiled doors.

You peeled back the skin of the earth
to a red that is closer to black,
you robbed everyday of its colours
of its softness, hardness and roundness,
its changes of leaves and of water,
its solidity of doors and of trees.
Our days are as thin as paper,
our nights cling wrap the darkness.

Blue girl -
you danced too close to the edge,
trying to keep your balance
right at the rim of the world.

Darkness

He fled from the noise and feasting
to hunt for you in the darkness.
Isn't that where you want him to be
outside with you in the darkness?

How can he enjoy the feast
when dark presses against the window?
How can he pull down the blind
on the shrieking silence outside?

Outside, with the bereft and broken,
the tortured, excluded, betrayed;
outside in the pain-filled darkness,
surely that's where you are.

He presses his face to the window:
he sees you, inside, at the table,
eating and drinking and laughing,
the life and soul of the party.

Service

as for me, the silence and the emptiness is so great, that I look and do not see, listen and do not hear — the tongue moves [in prayer] but does not speak ... I want you to pray for me — that I let Him have [a] free hand (attrib. Mother Teresa)

She saw him in the Calcutta street
knew his brown broken body
and understood in that brilliant moment
what she should do.

Years pass; duty hardens;
all the glimmering shades of skin
fade to one
sludge of suffering.

She holds to her bond
but regards them as animals,
only in death calls them angels,
no longer sees humans.

Why is she forsaken?
Is it all a terrible mistake?
Was that skewering moment of love
a trick of the blood?

Dutifully, her tongue moves
but her unspoken words are unanswered;
in the blind silence, obediently
she waits in the dark.

Imaginary Friend

Mine, of course, is male
and I'll never betray him
although I'm afraid of the truth drug
and what I may say on the table;
lately, however, I think
perhaps it's he who is leaving.

I have made up a code for his story:
scratched out hieroglyphics
no-one will ever decipher
etched on the inside of my head;
there like a comfort blanket
too tattered to be washed or aired.

He moves with the times and seasons,
though never much past forty
and he has no mobile phone;
he is unspecifically handsome
and that tiny twitch of the lips,
is a smile only I can imagine.

Funeral homily

What I heard was
'the frozen wings of angels'
so far beyond
whatever any of us
purgatory heaven - hell
was never mentioned
nor either side of suffering
but the delay

as angels hover
shivering
held by the burden
of icy feathers
waiting for
perfection.

Just a Cigar

Sometimes a cigar is just a cigar;
sometimes, a secret killer
that grabs at the throat
that chokes in the night.

Sometimes a fast car is just a Ferrari:
explosion in the eardrums
pounding red blood,
the roar of the crowd.

Sometimes a train is just inter-city;
sometimes, a softnosed bullet
dumdumming the darkness:
sirens, blue lights.

Sometimes a snake is just a snake
slithering through grass
minding its own business
under the apple trees.

V

Days in April

(all titles are taken from the poems of W.S. Graham)

The Sea as Metaphor of the Sea

Tell that to the marines
or the sea-logged refugees
whose leaky boats
hardly crest the waves
on this outlawed channel
so desperately cast on

where every pitch and trough
intake exhale of breath
seesaw of the heart
and every peak's the moment
before the wave's swallow
is every moment
and sea is
the metaphor of sea.

The Hide and Seeking Streets

Ilford's where I'm looking
first for a Ladies' toilet
then some kind of sandwich
before the funeral;
I'm walking through the mall
but all the shops are hiding
disguised, the shops are closed.

I'm looking for the graveyard
but all the flames are hiding
decorous in heavy velvet curtains;
afterwards, still hungry
I'm looking for the words
but all my words are hiding
disguised, are idle chat.

Those I Like Who are Dead

stand jabbering silently
on the shores of Acheron;
they have no understanding
and whatever they are now
is quite beyond me;
even so, more often recently,
I bat my questions at their reflective quiet
too late, come bouncing back

and if I'd saved their letters
the answers wouldn't correspond
to what I'm asking now;
but those illustrious ones,
dust and ashes also, left words
which sometimes speak.

Curious Necessary Space

My grandson is non-verbal
curled up behind the wall
his beast is there asleep
but not asleep in silence
it grunts and snorts and moans
he prods it into dancing
at the abstract heart of words
it hears the sound of music;

and we send words across
a different kind of distance;
stood at his foggy window
he sends us blurry signs
from a language Legoland
where his beast still stamps on syntax.

Always Language is where the People are

But what when language fails us?
or do we fail the language
like some terrible exam
that passes us as human?

When words refuse to come
or hide in strange disguises,
when dancing shapes in air
those recombining patterns
no longer yield their sense
to ear or eye or lips or fingertips;

on the strand of wordlessness
are those people still our people
whom language has forgotten
whom we tend with careful terror?

The Poetry Arm

Today was all left-handed.
I've slapped it on the wrist,
wrapped what it's written, hidden
in a file, locked behind a password:
a little bomb of bitterness
I couldn't post online.

My left hand's the clumsy one
blundering on the truth,
galumphing after images
through fences I keep closed.

I've shut my left hand up;
my right hand keeps my counsel
on that place across the road,
the house I married into.

Don't let Master Cat out

Who is not, of course, a real cat
but, like a real cat, scratches morosely
at the kitchen door.
He wants to get out, prowl the night,
yowl on garden walls
he wants to taunt and pounce and bite
and if you keep him buttoned up
just there below your sternum

you'll get a shocking belly-ache
he'll sink his abstract teeth
into your true-love's hand
and with his non-existent claws
he'll rip and shred
your pulsing heart.

Wisps of April

Snow today – and yes,
the snow was real, but still
I went out walking
In these pandemic times
another day of walking
to make the poem up.

My damsons are in flower,
the swans are on the lake
but their cygnets are all gone;
the white-faced coot is taking
a yellowed iris leaf,
like a ribbon, to its nest

and I'm grateful for the words
we have to say these things.

The Words We Breathe and Puff

Tonight the sky is absolutely wordless,
not a puff of an airy nothing
interrupts its insouciant blue;
trees on the roadside lean in
confidentially, and the dark ponder
of pines this evening is genial;
the motorway, like a flat sentence
rolls out perfectly punctuated
but finally anticlimactic.
                              Imagine
a world that is speechless
a world without humans or made things
a world where whatever there is
is naked, expressed only
in terms of itself.

The Edge of the Poem

How much more often than thrice
the cockerel on the other allotments
has crowed over my betrayals.
This slotting of words into place
is abashed as reality spools out
beyond any fix of language.

The people inside my head
can be inconstant and insincere;
they play with the colours of vocables
like children with a bucket of Lego
beguiled by the bricks' sweet click
unconcerned when the thing they've made
though it is itself a new thing
bears no relation to reality.

Walk the Dead Water

'Deep water! Sinking mud!'
'Stay on the boardwalk.'
It's the water that's sinking
under the gaze of a glowering sun;

the swan breasts a carpet of green scum
on the channels into the kingfisher pond;
no kingfisher, but a single duckling
is all his parents can show to the world.

Would a good shower of rain fix it?
or has the run-off from overfed fields,
too many pills flushed into the water,
robbed the nests, clogged the streams?

How can words fix it? How can words
lift the rank stink from the meadow?

Real Unabstract Snow

Take, for instance, snow:
the single flake that melts on cheek
before tongue tastes, and snow
much more rarely now the regular returner
to Alpine slope and polar icecap.

Snow the word is real, a sound
mouth shapes, that ink can make on paper
as *dodo* is a word and *hippogriff*
though those are magic spellbook words
abstracted from the world.

Severed from its substance, *snow*
Is just a word, there to conjure up
what isn't real, except as memory
or what might be imagined.

The Wanderlusting Sky of Morning

The sky neither lusts nor wanders
though underneath it we do
and sky provides horizons
that twin with sea and forest,
mountain, hill or moorland -
the distance eye demands,
the open invitation
heart is lusting for;

but the ones whose windows frame
bricks and blocks of housing
where sky is just a guess
locked out behind the buildings,
how can they imagine
a morning they might wander?

Tarnished Ticker

How is your ticker doing?
How do you think or feel
with your ear against the pillow
when you hear those numbered beats?

How is your noggin doing?
Do you count your words and days,
sort your papers out,
remember what to write?

How are you on your pins?
Can you still get about,
climb your seven Munros,
make it to your gate?

Watch out! you're losing time.
Hurry! before you're timeless.

Tenses are Everywhere

The poet writes about the dead girl:
the black dyslexic boy has drawn her portrait
beautifully, although his father doesn't want
him to be an artist; remembering in words
brings back the present. She was difficult
a naughty girl who slept with half-fledged soldiers
a clever ignorant girl, afraid to fail
and so she fell

out of her past into the artist's present;
what she did is in the simple past
what she did before that is pluperfect;
'what if', 'if only', and 'could have been'
here with us in our repeat rehearsals,
no future now, only past and present.

The Behaviour of Silence

I find silence hard to believe in,
death perhaps, even then
the rustle and shifts of decay.
This evening down on the allotments
I'm alone, but it's very noisy,
the chink of keys in my pocket
clunkety-clack of the freight train
birds on their evening playlist.

Behaviour of silence for you
is the abjuration of words
but the words go on in your head
yours or the gods', what difference,
better than the blare of the radio
the silencing sound of the news.

The Other Side of Language

It is snowing, just a little, from a clear sky
like messages from elsewhere, beyond interpretation:
over there, across the river spate
over there, beyond the barbed and booby-trapped
border wire, or there behind the wall
topped with broken glass and neither gap nor gate,
or there, dividing one from one,
the language shredder, double-bladed sword.

What is the other side, who or where
we want to get to, occupy or kill?
Pursuing the impossible translation
that will lift us, take us over,
we look to the sky again
but the messages have melted.

Rank-breathed at my elbow

I don't see them; even in sunlight
their darkness overlaps my shadow
but the smell is more or less always
rank, whether life or mortality;
the jabber jabber of voices
is garbled, incomprehensible
like radio calls from beleaguered cities
fogged in the hiss of static.
Another terrible exam
where I'm required to pass as interpreter
but the headphones aren't working properly
I haven't studied those languages
and I know I'll be damned by failure
because all I can hear is pain.

This is a Public Place

Yesterday into my living room
a boy wearing a stripey teeshirt
as ordinary as Next or Primark
brought with him his landscape of sand;
the goat he carried was starving
and the space in public he opened
was wider than I can find words for.

Today in a glade of rewilding
words are pinned up for the public:
notifications of kingfisher and coltsfoot
but the words don't keep their promises,
there are degradations and diminutions
and the bird that chides from the treetop
refuses to give me its name.

Children Flying

I can remember flying
like cygnets leaving early
above my uncle's car
his dark green dashing Riley;
I true or false remember
when almost half asleep
how to push off with one foot
float past their gaping faces;

like the magic bewitched children
swans with human voices
who flew around the lake
until she stitched their little shirts
trapped them as they rested
brought them down to earth.

The Wrecked Dragon

My father kept a dragon under the hill
behind his house though it wasn't
his own dragon, and he
wasn't my biological father;
he never showed it to me
but I saw the key in his attic
when I climbed there
through a long tunnel of books.

I went out one day to find it
into the hills on horseback;
I saw nothing except for a haze
that might have been dragon's breath
hiding the huts of a vanished people
who lived under its scaly wings.

The Net of Light

Reticulated patterns on the sand
under blue and green waters
fish untrammelled swim through;
a lacery of branches holds the light
casts its shadowy network
and all of this though nothing
is a hammock holds me up
is a safety net delights me.

My strawberry net ensnared
entangled, trapped a female blackbird;
through thick protective gloves
I felt her beating heart;
the unresisting seabed
is scraped and scoured by nets.

Sleeping Alone Together

There's a crazy man on the headland
staring at the scribbled sea
paying out lines of syntax
and talking to himself

all night long he's afraid
to go back to his lonely bed
where his words aren't her words
where she curls away from him

round the kernel of herself;
he puts his trust in the mind's ear
the voice only he can hear
hauls in his catch

of silvery slippery shiny things
and takes them home to her.